T0365866

Dr. Locandro comments on *WILDEGEEST!* Sequel:
"A friendly upbeat road map to bring you to 89 years of age with
good health and a great
attitude towards life, society and the need to care for others.
An eclectic conglomeration
of food facts for life from a uniquely educated person. Ted has placed in
proper perspective what and how we should eat - read between the
lines -listen to what he says - it works! . . .
Ted is quite a man for his age. I have 23 years to catch up.
I hope I can still drive
4000 miles, round trip to Newfoundland, be as healthy as he is, and run
a continuous dialogue with an anthropomorphized canine partner."
Roger R. Locandro, Ph.D., professor emeritus
RUTGERS, the State University of New Jersey

The book, *WILDEGEEST! A Search for Last Places,* was gradually recorded
on the World Wide Web www.wildegeest.com as the author, identified as
"the man," ably assisted by almost-blind dog Dora, and then "bestfrienddog"
Theodore www.bestfrienddog.com, traveled four hundred
thousand miles on a thirteen-
year odyssey, which resulted in important conclusions concerning the aging
process and the rights of the elderly.

This entire illustrated book of 325 pages has now been reedited and recorded
on CD, in a format that can be easily read on most computers without going
on-line. In this digitally published *Sequel,* "the man" suggests a long-range
program that *persons near fifty* should undertake in order to have a long life
and rewarding old age as their ultimate aim.

Wildegeest!
A Search for Last Places

Sequel: He found Newfoundland (His photos tell why)

A Longevity Guide for People Near Fifty
(Never Let Life Put a Leash on You)
by
Ted Miller and bestfrienddog Theodore

www.wildegeest.com
www.bestfrienddog.com

WILDEGEEST!

A Search for Last Places

Ted M. Miller
Text & Photography

Lorne Warren
Technical Consultant

Gerry Lavery
Editor
&
Theodore
bestfrienddog

Sequel -He found Newfoundland

WILDEGEEST!

A Search for Last Places—Sequel
The Players

Ted M. Miller (Identified herein as "the man")
and
Theodore (bestfrienddog)

T a b l e   o f   C o n t e n t s

ILLUSTRATIONS
Photos in this Sequel are the man's chosen views
of the Northern Peninsula of Newfoundland,
by far, his favorite "Last Place"

8

PREFACE

A WHOOP AND A HOLLER FROM FIFTY?

If you're near fifty, ignore this book at your own risk! For if you drift into a thoughtless, unregulated approach to aging, then the likely outcome will be early senility and loneliness.

A frequent lament from middle-aged readers of *WILDEGEEST! A Search for Last Places,* "Oh, I wish my mother/father could read this." To which the author replies, "Sorry, this ain't a book for them who's blown it. It's for healthy-minded people with enough savvy, guts and spine to dodge the fatuous pathways that led their elders astray. Even then, there must be enough maturity and character to seriously embark upon and continue a program that can extend your life and make it productive throughout."

In the book, and now in the sequel, the author identifies himself as "the man." At 76, his wife's death left him shattered and disoriented. He then combined inner disciplines and resources with the instinctive will to survive, and embarked on a completely different lifestyle. This has given him thirteen additional, meaningful years, and a strong desire to share his life-extending approach with others.

He relied heavily on the companionship of retired housedog Dora, then Theodore (see www.bestfrienddog.com), in sharing enjoyment of nature, constant physical activity, and good nutrition.

Equally important was the constant pursuit of challenging worthwhile projects,
much of which he described with flare, humor, and imaginary tales that outrageously imitate Jonathan Swift's *Gulliver's Travels.*

For a number of years, the story of how the man and his dogs created a whole new life was reported in fits and starts on the World Wide Web at www.wildegeest.com. Now this website has been reedited and formatted in book form, and recorded on CD. Simply place the disk in your computer and you can read the entire illustrated book without going on-line.

"Hey elderly goofus!" the man's friends respectfully ask, "ain't you strained weary gentle readers' eyeballs enuf? What's this *Sequel* thang?"

The budding *Sequel* writer wearily replies, "Mind yer words, 'bys, or I'll wrap yer bodes 'round thet prickly tree, an' tie yer floppy ears into grannyknots."

At the tender age of eighty-seven, the man indeed thought the book complete. But he soon realized that even the most dedicated readers do not comprehend, or wish to accept, much of what he wishes to convey.

So now the man shinnies up a convenient tree stump, faces his imaginary readers, and teeter-tottering as he shouts, "LET ME MAKE MYSELF PLAIN!"

"PLAINLY," declaims the man, "a skilled inquisitor is needed to ask leading questions that will reveal what this Sequel is about. So get the show on the road, worthy Interrogator, query at will!"

Q.   What makes you think YOU are qualified to tell middle-aged folks how to plan their future?

A.   I agree, noble Inquirer, it sounds presumptuous, when there are so many health publications that offer professional advice. But scratch the surface and you may discover recommendations permissive enough to accommodate special interests. Some of the loopholes are big enough to drive a soda pop truck through. Survival may depend upon ability to select safe, sensible, protective and healing foods in the supermarket.

Empty calories must be avoided. Worshipers of the well-advertised nutrition pyramid should be warned that it is much less valid if supported by white flour rather than a whole grain foundation. With so many bad eating habits extant in the land, small wonder the hooked-on-fast-foods population gets fatter, flabbier, and less likely to have a long productive life.

Q. So you presume to be Czar Cure-all at the dinner table?

A. If I could, I'd start with young children, upon whom the sins of the moms and pops are imprinted. Careless eating fills early graves. Since the stakes are high, people must not be allowed to forget the importance of protective and healing foods. As the message becomes ingrained, they will find it easier to turn away from the "no-no" foods that cram the supermarkets.

But man/woman doesn't survive on whole-wheat bread alone. The most devastating roadblock to a healthy advanced old age transition is that distasteful word, AGEISM (with such equivalents as age discrimination, class hatred, social prejudice).

Q. Do you think you have out-thought and out-flanked the scores of books on aging and its prejudices?

A. Aye! I combed libraries, *ad nauseam,* and found little that was supportive or reassuring. If anything, disparity between the young and the old has worsened in the last fifty years. Many oldsters prefer mingling with their "kind." Their incomes determine selection of communities ranging from cushy to substandard, with games the only assured diversion.

Enlightenment requires hands-on experience that has not been widely applied to persons in their late-late years. I found Simone de Beauvoir's book, *The Coming of Age,* gathering dust in a used book store; a real treasure that applies just as well today. It was translated from the French and published by G. P. Putman's Sons in 1972. A few selected lines from the introduction:

"When I say I am working on a study of old age -- people generally exclaim, 'What an extraordinary notion! . . . but you aren't old! . . . what a dismal subject.'

"And that is indeed the very reason why I am writing this book. I mean to break the conspiracy of silence."

I had much the same thought when I dedicated the *WILDEGEEST!* book to the "Unseen Majority." This *Sequel* is intended to bring the Unseen Majority into view. My qualifications are impeccable. Invisibility increases as you work your way through the Arctic eighties. I have traveled this time zone and remain coherent enough to speak my piece.

Q. What about other missing links in this unfinished saga, such as the EarthWise Farm project?

A. Completion of the *WILDEGEEST!* story left me wondering. What could Theodore and I do now? When we returned to the "home place" in North Carolina, the beautiful farm I had purchased long ago from Mr. Ken Parker had recently been used to grow cotton, and was reeking of chemicals.

Intolerable! Development and land purchases were closing in, demolishing the farmers. It was time to hold the line and clean up the soil, demonstrate pesticide-free growing of vegetables, fruits and grains.

Now in its third year, EarthWise Farm has earned favorable comments, but no voluntary labor or dedicated neighbors. "I may be fifty years late," muses the man, "the world changes."

"The changes and chances of this mortal life," commented Shakespeare.

Q. Now the 64,000 kopek question. You've searched thirteen years for "Last Places." What have you found?

A. The illustrations in this *Sequel* are the answer. The island of Newfoundland offers beauty, relaxation, activities in every direction. Here a person learns to enjoy the small as well as the outsized magnificent views. This is a friendly place where people of all ages can be relaxed and comfortable.

DOGGEREL

Theodore's thoughts drift fog-like into the computer's "Word Perfect." "What a long duty tour my life has been! Soon I'll be nine dog-eared years old, the best half of those years spent in Newfoundland, where me and the man own a cabin.

"I feel uncomfortable when these egotistical humans multiply my age by seven. In some mysterious way they think this puts my life span on a human level. My paw-key calculator informs me that nine times seven is SIXTY-THREE! How shocking! I'm like a sixty-three-year-old man? I'll believe it when I see *him* chase a moose half a mile through tangled brush.

"Consider this. I've had to share this man's diet and lifestyle in most ways. But not when he bounds out of his bunk at 5:00 A.M., or sunup, whichever comes first, hungry as a bear and drooling for breakfast. Is this what humans do to live a full life? Can it work for me? Let me paw the calculator. How many dogged years must I nurse this guy until he's one hundred?

"I recently asked him to define the word sequel. He explained that words frequently have many meanings, and in this instance sequel means following. I nearly bit his arm, 'Yea Dude'," I growled, teeth showing, "following also means trailing, hounding, dogging and heeling; let me remind you! Years ago I taught you never to use demeaning dog-dogma words in my presence."

"Furthermore," I howled, "how many times must I repeat? LIFE IS NEVER GOING TO PUT A LEASH ON ME."

Take a lesson from wise old dog, Theodore. People who are about fifty years old can still hope for many years of active life. But it will only happen enjoyably if there is recognition that hard places and roadblocks do indeed lie ahead. Be a good scout, "Be Prepared."

VAGABONDAGE

"I was a six week old pup when I first met Dora," recalls Theodore. "She was upset when the man told her to be my 'nanny', because she thought it meant' goat'." But then her maternal instincts kicked in and before long her loving care caused memories of my mother and father to fade. I do recall their fur was red, while twelve-year-old golden retriever Dora's was a washed-out blond.

"Dora's tales gave me an inkling of what my future held. Her role as a housedog had ended abruptly when Sylvia, her favorite person, was no longer there. At first glance not a promising teammate for high adventure, except for her sea legs on their sailboat in all kinds of weather.

"So there she was, eyesight failing, daily routine a shambles, and now with a shattered old man on her hands.

"'Dora,'" said the man, "only one thing to do: Stand up, stiffen backbones, find a new way to live. I'll be your 'seeing-eye man'; your nose and ears must forewarn us of dangers. Time to head out!'

"What a new life they found!" marvels Theodore, "for details you must read the book, but I do recall some exciting tales: They crossed the Rio Grande in a Mexican's flimsy boat, paddling furiously to avoid being swept into a canyon; they were lost in the snow near Grand Canyon, Colorado; they camped above the Arctic Circle in the Yukon; they were trapped in mud near an Alaskan glacier in Alaska; they spent two days crossing Labrador on an unfinished gravel road.

"But most important, they discovered the bonding of man and dog," says Theodore. "Dora died when I was still too much a strong-willed, opinionated pup to understand the heavy responsibilities I was to assume."

A few years later, the man's daughter Jenny and her friend Jane arranged a weekend exhibition in their art studios in Hillsborough, North Carolina. It featured his paintings, collages, travel tales and artifacts. Theodore was introduced to each visitor as the star. There were raised eyebrows and quizzical expressions as the man tried to explain his deep indebtedness to Dora and Theodore. But his judgment was vindicated and agreed upon by dozens of travelers he met along the way. In just about every instance he observed how closely dogs of every description were bonded to *their* humans.

The exhibition received favorable reviews, and suggestions that a book was needed to explain its relevance to long life and happiness. This was the incentive that started the man's narrative and its being recorded on the Internet; the details determined by his lively imaginary characters, his "tru-lyin' adventures," and the actual memorable events that occurred.

BRAIN POWER

"A Brain is a Terrible Thing to Waste," he read, as he sped past a highway sign that displayed a pitifully underfed child.

That vast population of neglected children whose minds and potential are wasted without sufficient nurturing!

"And what is *nurturing?"* pondered the man, "as applied to children, it means that all of them, rich or poor, require a full measure of *tender loving care, encouragement, nutrition, protection, support, and training."*

An important criteria for judging the success of a society is how it helps all of its young people cope with the modern world.

"Hey man," barks Theodore, "you're kinda off track. This *Sequel* features people near fifty, not children."

"Shut your muzzle, Bowzer," replies the man, "since you question my astute observations, I assure you my thoughts also apply to puppy dogs unfortunate enough to be adopted by families who ignore the nurturing process. Neglected dogs develop personality and learning disorders, and the blighters who neglect them do not hesitate to cruelly cast them aside."

"Your remarks," grins Theodore, "explain why I am a superior, highly respected, beloved dog, and master of the house. Can it be the *au naturel* food we eat?"

"I'll discuss diet later, and at length," replies the man, "but I must remind you that the fish we frequently consume has been called a 'brain food'. The omega-3s in fish oils undoubtedly play an active role in keeping the brain and eyes up to par.

"Which reminds me of when I skillfully plied my trade as a 'fish chemist,'" recalls the man, "and was sent to attend an international conference on the benefits of fish oils in dealing with cardiovascular diseases."

The delegates' pithy discussions regarding greasy fish fat effects on the heart and circulatory system were interrupted by a delegate who suggested that they should also consider how these lipids effect the head.

"The chair said he was disruptive and out of order," recalls the man. "Since I too had wondered how fish fats effect everything from toenails to brains, I longed to spring to his defense and tell that overly focused group, 'Brothers, Sisters, what th' guy sez is true! Like that old song say, *"th' head bone is connected to th' body bone, and the body bone is connected to th' heart bone, YEAH YEAH !"*

By now the most devoted readers wonder where this gobbledygook is leading. Is the man's head bone disconnected?

"Naturellement - not!" bellows the man, "these anecdotes, and my comments concerning children, etcetera, can tell us much about how human society functions and malfunctions, and can remind us of attitudes which most people choose to ignore. As to my reminiscences, retrospection is an established privilege of the ancients, whose narratives can be beneficially soothing, sleep inducing, and at times may contain a useful tidbit for the human psyche, *anima humana.*

"As one's age progresses through the dangerous 'sixties, the defensive 'seventies, and the barren 'eighties, the availability of human warmth, an adult form of mutual nurturing, becomes increasingly tenuous.

"In this rarified atmosphere, a person develops an unhealthy interest in medications, especially for those diseases that seemed inherent to people *stricken in years.*

"Seems to me," muses the man, "when I was young, during the hardship days, advertising was much more ethical and truthful."

"Oh my!" whines Theodore, "another long-winded story about how hard he worked for a dollar a day."

"Heck, Theodore, sometimes I earned twice that much! But I do recall that government agencies monitored advertising claims with greater care," replies the man. "On one occasion, our laboratory unsuccessfully defended a client's advertised claims concerning his denture adhesive. The judge stated his firmly held opinion that the denture adhesive was worthless. As he read the verdict, his denture plates waggled loosely and failed to keep up with his lips.

"Alcoholic snake-bite cures - horse liniments for arthritis - mustard poultices for chest colds - castor oil for almost everything! All relatively harmless cures compared with present-day pharmaceutical hype, and press releases that provide false hope without adequate proof.

"Assuredly, it's a slippery slope if you allow yourself to drift unprepared into the aging process," says the man, "and a hyperactive interest in medications and medical treatments is an inauspicious way to prepare for later years. So is a lackadaisical belief that society will recall your worth, deeds and awards, after you enter those frosty latitudes.

"So, you plus-or-minus-fifty-year-old people, now is the time to shape up and ship out on a wonderful, unique adventure -- to make a careful assessment of your lifestyle and decide how you must correct your course, and what must be taken aboard for a safe long voyage into the future.

"But I warn you, shipmates," says the man, "this voyage requires brain power every step of the way, and there's a prevailing belief that brains deteriorate with time, in spite of our best efforts. Admittedly, some diseases are a constant hazard, threatening us from off stage. But there's a better chance that such disasters will not occur.

"The usual scenario is 'softening of the brain' through mismanagement. Your body becomes soft and flaccid when physical exercise is neglected, and so does your brain if it is not given a continuous flow of challenges.

"Can you continue to do only what 'turns you on'?" asks the man, rhetorically.

"Sorry, chums, it's going to take a lot more than that. Fun and games are recreation, not the road to a long, meaningful life. If you want to safeguard your place in this world, start long term projects, or accept volunteer assignments that require heavy-duty thinking, then hang on with the skin of your teeth, or with your modern glued-in dentures, or with your bare gums, and never let go."

Mackenzie,
Born in Nain, Labrador

BODYGUARD

Before NASA reached Mars, Edgar Rice Burroughs (1875-1950) convinced his many fans that exciting life flourished on the fourth planet. Included was a race of brainy spider-like creatures, with weak legs, who used headless humans for transport.

A perfect symbiotic arrangement! Such brainy creatures would not allow their trusty steeds to be anything but strong and healthy. Earthlings do the same for their million-dollar horses.

But when the brain is comfortably encompassed in its ivory tower, attached firmly to the body, it frequently ignores the creaks and burbles of its transport system, and neglects to synapse orders for its care and maintenance.

"So stop horsing around, and start feeling your oats!" advises the man.

"For you have reached the critical fifties, a transition point, where a long life as a mature viable person should be planned for and counted on, or you can opt for *laissez-faire-ism* (inertia, immobility, vegetation), a greater chance that you will become part of the *unseen majority,* and shorten your sentient life.

"It takes *guts* to grab control and embark on the former course," says the man, "and the healthy, functioning gut, an absolute essential for a long life, consists of the mouth, esophagus, stomach, the liver-gallbladder-pancreas functions, the small intestine, and the large intestine.

"It is important to note that feces, eliminated as result of healthy digestion, contains about one-third bacteria. While residing in the bowel, organisms play an essential role by generating Vitamins B12 and K, completing the breakdown of proteins, and being fueled by hard-to-digest complex carbohydrates," explains the man. "It's a fortuitous relationship! These *good bacteria* are sorely missed when antibiotics decimate their ranks. For similar reasons, I avoid foods laced with preservatives that may inhibit their growth."

Statistics that demonstrate food consumption patterns and other undisciplined lifestyles make it obvious that most people subject their digestive systems to frightful abuse. This helps explain why there is so much need for medical intervention."

"Yeah man," whines Theodore, "you've never allowed me to have the manufactured foods that most dogs eat, so I've had to depend on your cooking, willing or unwilling, for my entire life."

"Don't sweat it, Theodore. I've kept you off canine 'fast foods' to protect your digestive system from chemical additives, empty calories, questionable fats and feed ingredients. As an alternative, you've had to belly up to foods which I select carefully, and cook with much regard for our gut reactions.

"When I take you to veterinarians," continues the man, "it's only to show them your white teeth, excellent health, and uninhibited personality.

"But to knock you down a peg, Theodore, I must remind you that it is me, not you, who is bright eyed, bushy tailed, and starving at first dawn," crows the man, "and as a result of good foods and careful cooking, I am sharply aware of flavors, odors and textures. I firmly believe that healthy, active old people have almost the same nutritional demands and food preferences as younger adults, in spite of many statements that tend to segregate them.

"And dogs are frequently tarred with the same brush," he continues. "People who feed the same manufactured dog food, day in and day out, believe their canines are without concern for variety. Untrue! If a complete dinner for humans is arranged in separate portions on a platter for Theodore, he will meticulously sniff each offering, then eat the foods in order of preference.

"Therein lies a message for everyone. Theodore has learned to like foods that are judged best for him. People can make the same transitions. Abandon foods that shorten lives, or cause debilitating conditions. Then, you can deliberately alter your eating patterns. There will be satisfaction in knowing that you are thereby protecting your health, and acquiring beneficial eating pleasures.

"I'll soon tell you about some foods that are likely to keep you young, healthy, and *active*," promises the man. "As for the latter, you must not delay in starting the *active role* -- vigorous walking combined with thinking, an activity you should continue, rain or shine, as an integral part of your daily routine, to be continued with ever-increased vigor for as long as you are able. Something like brushing your teeth on a regular basis, only more important, since your whole being is involved.

"If you decide to give this combined mental/physical exercise your serious attention, you'll soon become increasingly fit and limber. Each day serious walking will help you think and plan constructively, and make you more attentive to the world around you.

"At the beginning, this recommended *mind-and-body exercise regimen* should not be allotted too large a share of your present lifestyle, since that would lead to its abandonment. In my opinion, it should be started on a very modest basis, gradually expanded and continued until it becomes a lifelong habit. When bolstered with suitable dietary changes, it can become your lifeline when you are older, an insurance policy worth keeping."

Most Northern part of Newfoundland
Viewed from Cape Norman Lighthouse

FOODSTUFFS

"Ahoy, Mates," cries the man, "to navigate uncharted fluidity and reach latitudes eighty, ninety, and away out yonder, you gotta hang in there, and hang tough.

"Need I remind you," sighs the man, "that the world is full of good intentions, but sooner or later we face our destinies quite alone?

"No matter how long this single-handed voyage, it can provide a unique opportunity for mature perception of new vistas, undimmed by old age."

"Gadzooks, Ancient Mariner!" barks Theodore, as he wolfs down an entire whole-grain-flour pancake, "how much jawbone is needed to shanghai folks aboard an extended cruise? Tell us the good stuffs - the food stuffs."

"Aye aye, BowWowZer," replies the man, "time we told 'em the kind of fuel a warm body needs for the long haul, but you ate my 'Made from Live Hard Wheat Kernels' exhibit.

"I don't plan to reinvent the wheel," says the man, "but I'm going to bet on *SEEDS* - like the ones that kept humans moving before they replaced backpacking.

"When I was a boy, people shopped for 'staples'-- a raw material, or commodity, grown or manufactured nearby. There wasn't much variety, but we enjoyed satisfying meals. Diseases and obesity, that are now endemic due to overabundance, were not much in evidence during the great depression of the '30s, or World War II rationing.

"Much could be gained if people with unused land, regardless of size, would reinvent 'Victory Gardens' as a way to add clean, fresh, nutritious vegetables and herbs to their daily food supply, and as a long-term continuing project. Two years ago I started 'EarthWise Farm', and banned pesticides and herbicides. We are now growing vegetables, fruits, and grains successfully.

"If you want your mind and body to be ready for the long haul, you must try to avoid chemical contaminants, and other stresses that injure your body, while you are still strong and active. Somehow, the tensions of daily life must

Theo helps Howard
Guard St. Anthony Airport

be compartmentalized to reduce the size and intensity of each irritant. Work- and sports-induced damage to joints and muscles, and poisons entering lungs in the work place and in smog-laden urban areas, should be avoided.

"But the greatest stress imposed upon most of the population is overeating of the wrong foods that are damaged by cooking methods. Everything you eat should be completely biodegradable.

"This sounds uncomfortably like a detergent ad," admits the man, "'Guaranteed not to damage the environment'. Quite appropriate, since foods entering a healthy digestive system should be readily reduced to toxin-free nutrients; and the residues eliminated with a sigh, not a groan."

"Oh me, oh my!" whines Theodore, "you're gonna scare th' livin' daylights out of these folks and make 'em abandon ship."

"No, Theodore, I'm about to propose a 'life raft' which they can board When ready," replies the man. "It's a suggested list of nourishing, protective, potentially healing foods for a 'longevity diet'. Some of the live seeds are not readily available and may have to be ordered by health food stores."

"Live seeds?" barks Theodore, "you've gone too far! I'm a canine, not a bird. Must I refer my case to the ASPCA?"

"A moment ago you wolfed down a delicious pancake, made from wheat seeds and home-grown buckwheat seeds, both ground into flour, and flax seeds shredded with a coffee grinder, and I heard no complaints," replies the man.

"Commercial milling of wheat produces a host of products, which include whole wheat flour, bleached white flour, wheat germ, and wheat gluten. Oxidation takes its toll, so if you attempted to restore the original grain, by mixing the fractions back together, it would no longer have the same nutrient potential.

"Like Humpty-Dumpty, all the kings horses, and all our 'enrichments', cannot restore that seed to its wondrous self.

"Logic advises us to trust a packaging system devised by nature, that keeps seeds alive and unchanged, and to use them in recipes without delay.

Theo checks Warren's operation
of Cape Norman Lighthouse.
(Fifth generation lighthouse keeper)

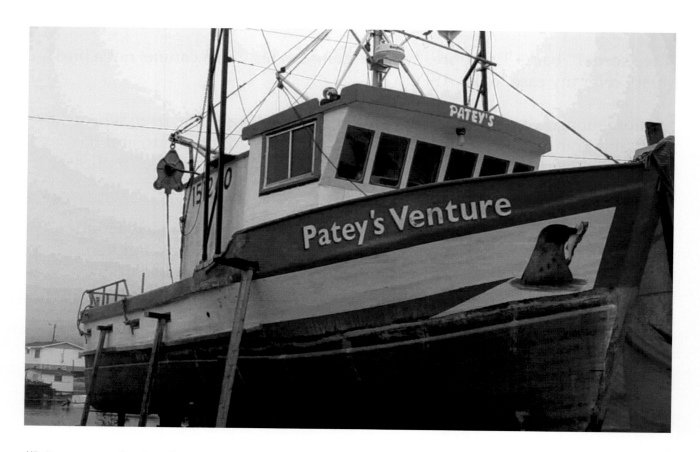

"Many seeds, in their pristine form, contain essential fatty acids that can complement the omega-3 benefits of fish oils. A suitable combination of seeds can also match meat and dairy proteins by supplying all of the essential amino acids that the body requires, and important vitamins and minerals as well."

"I know what's coming," says Theodore. "Guess I'll slip outside, sniff around, and munch grass, while you tell these folks about ingredients that make my jaws ache for a sun-cured moose bone."

The man turns to his imaginary audience and launches his favorite tirade, *"BREAD cannot possibly be the staff of life if it's made of bleached white flour.* Wheat kernels and other seeds, when ground into flour and made into breads, pancakes and pastas, can indeed provide the sturdy staff required for a long life.

"And now a *disclaimer,* before I say more about what's good for you," says the man. "Obviously, not all things are good for all people. Certain vegetables and fruits may have curative powers when eaten specifically to confront certain physical conditions. Many people cannot 'handle' certain foods, due to adverse reactions. So, dear friends, while my food selections are intended to put brakes on your shopping list, you must still ask your doctor, or seek other professional advice, if therapeutic objectives are involved.

"The USDA Food Guide Pyramid provides flexible nutritional guidelines applicable to many people, but not sufficiently specific for most. Many rearrangements of the Pyramid are needed if you are an honest-to-goodness vegan; or a vegetarian (V) who eats seafood; or a (V) who eats poultry; or a(V) who avoids red meat, but eats poultry and seafood; or a (V) who occasionally eats red meats, but pigs out on poultry and seafood. Obviously, each of these requires redesign of the pyramid to make it valid, and none of it has meaning if the food ingredients are not fully described.

"One way that product descriptions mislead is by underestimating portion sizes, as is frequently done with potato chips and crackers to make the fat and salt content appear acceptable. As to the latter, a suggested portion of five crackers might weigh 15 grams and contain 1.5 grams of vegetable shortening. Is a cracker with ten percent fat, the low-fat cracker the label says it is?

"Who claimed that ketchup is a vegetable, suitable for the school lunch program? The proposal must have come from lobbyists, intent on disposing of surpluses, including those which lure children away from simple nourishing fare. The original program was intended to feed each child, especially the poor ones, at least one nutritious meal, and a glass of milk, per day. Has the need lessened? Or has society decided it cannot stop this seduction of children's taste buds?

"Are children the only ones whose food consumption patterns have been altered? No indeed. Almost everyone has been victimized by this prolific abundance, this teemingness of choices, this galaxy of enhanced flavors and colors, and its readiness at every drive-in window.

"Aggressive marketing of thousands of food items, gross overconsumption and consequent larding of the population, is the government-approved way to keep the economy up and running."

The man solemnly asks, "Is this the civilized world that people want? How many are misled by this huge, glittering, outsized Trojan Horse and its ability to charm and distort the lives of large segments of the population: children, young adults, people near fifty, the aging, the old, and the very old?

"These observations suggest an important role for 'people near fifty'. They can set an example by shopping for foods that are undeniably good for them, and by ignoring the overburden of trash foods and beverages. There is strength in numbers. Food offerings should be based on the health-requirements of the customers, not the retailer's profit motives.

"Until customer resistance develops," laments the man, "your shopping lists will continue to be threatened, as you tread your way through these opulent bazaars crammed with tantalizing foods, strategically stacked for gravity-assisted transfer into your shopping cart.

"Halt!" shouts the man, "retreat, go home, sate your hunger, regroup and return. This time with a complete checklist of foods that can supply your actual dietary needs, probably about one hundred items. Then your purchases at the average supermarket will leave twenty thousand or more food items untouched.

"Come, my friends," says the man, "let's take another look at that USDA Food Guide Pyramid. Have you parked your Camel? Oh I'm so glad that you candidates for longevity have stopped smoking.

"This roomy bottom area represents foods you should eat each day (6 to 11 servings), to supply most of the caloric needs for care, maintenance, and expended energy. Breads, cereals, and pastas should contain whole grains as the predominant ingredient. As for the flours, please be sure to include whole wheat, rye, buckwheat, oats, corn meal, and unbleached white flour.

"Later, I'll discuss kitchen equipment for making your own fresh flours. Then your shopping list will include live seeds: barley, brown rice, buckwheat, corn, millet, oats, rye, and wheat. I have already mentioned the valuable fats and proteins these seeds can provide. There are also the beneficial fibers that assist digestion.

"Now look upward at the second-largest area, devoted to vegetables (3 to 5 servings per day) and to fruits (2 to 4 servings per day). I think you can thrive on lots of interchange between the two groups, and that low-calorie vegetables can be eaten ad lib to help you leave the table satiated.

"Should vegetables be eaten raw or cooked, to aid elimination? I think that salads and other raw vegetables should be eaten for other reasons, but that fresh fruits and certain cooked vegetables with fiber can contribute the required bulk and motility.

"Vegetables to consider for your shopping list include: asparagus, beets, broccoli, brussels sprouts, cabbage, cauliflower, celery, corn, cucumber, onions, okra, peas, peppers, potatoes, spinach, squash, sweet potatoes, tomato, turnip, plus an array of fresh herbs.

"Fruits to consider for your shopping list include: apple, apricots, avocado, blueberries, cherries, dates, figs, lemon, lime, melons, oranges, Kiwi fruit, pears, pineapple, prunes, raspberries, strawberries, and tropical fruits of various colors.

"Now we have reached the third level of the pyramid, which suggests milk, yogurt and cheese (2 to 3 servings) and meat, poultry, fish, dry beans, eggs, nuts group (2 to 3 servings).

Obediah samples
Pickled Herring

"This is an area where judgment and forbearance dictates your selections, especially in keeping consumption of red meats and high-fat cheeses tightly under control. Eggs are good for most people, but 'moderation' is the key word that governs their consumption. Chicken and turkey can be used in so many ways that they serve as satisfying alternates to animal meats. Low-fat yogurt and tofu now offer ways to add pizzazz to longevity diets.

"Keep these suggestions in mind and be sure to include wild, saltwater fish: herring, mackerel, salmon, sardines, tuna (fresh, frozen, or canned) for frequent use. Don't forget the canned or dried: black-eyed peas, chick peas, lima beans, kidney beans, and navy beans; and raw nuts, especially almonds, brazil nuts, walnuts.

"Now we have reached the small triangle at the top of the pyramid, devoted to fats, sweets, alcohol and salt, all to be used sparingly. I suggest much restraint in satisfying sweet tooth, and that you avoid sugar substitutes.

"You'll get most of the fats you require as part of ingredients already mentioned, so for limited needs, I suggest 'Extra Virgin Olive Oil, and butter."

"Hey man," barks Theodore, "your ingredients list makes me thirsty, what about water?"

"A bountiful supply of good water is an absolute requirement since a person should drink 6 to 8 glasses of water each day. If there is any doubt about the purity of the water supply, then you should consider bottled spring water from a reliable source.

"This has been a long shopping tour, and I'm plum tuckered. My dear readers are restlessly moving about, wondering how to use this pile of ingredients.

"Be of good cheer, me Hearties," says the man, "help is only a page away."

Gourmandize

"Galley slaves to the poop deck," shouts the man. "Now neophytes, never forget this, my most important cooking lesson."

"Oh my," whines Theodore, "half this middle-aged crew gonna jump ship, or throw that smart-assed old man overboard. Now, I gotta drag this canvas wrapped thang to th' poop deck."

"Thanks, Theodore, for delivering this killer-machine for deep-six burial," says the man. "If you're gonna pray, pray for the victims of the dearly departed.

"Drop it, dawg," screams the man. "Overboard!"

"There goes my deep fat fryer," moans one of the neophytes. "You said you'd use it to teach us something important. Now how will I fry those lovely potato strips I sliced for supper?"

"If you hope to complete the long haul, my friend, you'll learn other ways to cook potatoes," replies the man, "because frying is man's or woman's worst enemy.

"How I hate thee, Fat-stuffs, let me count the ways," sings the man. "Natural fats and oils are a useful, and even essential, part of the diet. But Fat-stuffs? That's my name for many of the refined oils, the shortening, and most butter substitutes. Hydrogenated fats contain undesirable trans fatty acids. As for those innocent-looking bottled oils, most carry a warning statement that heating to the smoke point is a fire hazard. But where is the warning that most are unsuitable for frying? When heated to frying temperatures, they undergo oxidative reactions which make them off-limits to anyone who longs for along life."

"Do you need a different cooking method?" Theodore asks the man, "I recall a tale about how cooking was invented. House burned down with a pig inside. Sounded yummy."

"Good try, Theodore. Charles Lamb wrote that essay," replies the man, "but I don't think everyday fare should be prepared by methods which overcook and char the meats of animals and birds.

"Much evidence warns us to avoid flame-charred meats, especially those with marbled fats. This kind of cooking reduces the availability of essential amino acids which are of primary importance. Pyrolysis of fats produces aldehydes, esters, ketones, and etceteras which may include carcinogens. On top of that, there are the undefined tars and residues from the flames."

"Who cares if amino acids are unemployed or available?" asks Theodore, "Don't rightly recall seeing, meeting, or eating one."

"Dumb dawg!" sneers the man, "amino acids are the building blocks of the proteins that have kept you lively alive, viably viable, and glossily furry. Obviously, your needs have been met. But I've seen what happens to chickens fed high-performance broiler diets containing heat-damaged protein.

"Cooked, pressed fish, carefully dried and ground into fish meal, is a source of protein in a broiler diet. If the fish meal is overheated or scorched during manufacture, its digestibility and the availability of its essential amino acids is reduced, and the rapidly growing chickens will not feather properly, a lysine deficiency called 'bareback'.

Mackenzie & Irene
Cow Head, Newfoundland

"Whilst digging up unpleasant memories," the man continues, "I hope Theodore never gets to see 'crazy chick disease' (encephalomalacia), caused by rancid fats. Can chickens provide warning signals for humans? This old man takes them seriously in selecting foods and cooking methods."

"I smell trouble in the fo'c's'le," sniffs Theodore, "gentle readers inquire what good's long life sans charred hamburgers and fries with that piquant acrolein flavor note?"

"Their livers may survive fast foods now and then. So it would be better 'then' than 'now'," replies the man.

"I admit, Theodore and I have at times succumbed to similar weaknesses, when the odor of Southern Fried Chicken wafted across the highway we were high-balling on.

"But the voice of experience must be heard," the man insists. "Since nineteen ninety, I have driven four hundred thousand miles and camped hundreds of times without a single dietary upset. Food selections and cooking methods must surely help explain the good health of man and dog.

"Dog and man travel on their stomachs," he proclaims, as he adopts a Napoleonic stance with one hand inside his jacket, "camping food selections were somewhat like those in the previous section. Vegetables were washed, water removed, packed in plastic bags, and kept in the cooler. Cut-up combinations of fresh fruits kept well when mixed with yogurt and refrigerated. Fat-free powdered milk was versatile, convenient, and space saving. A large supply of canned wild salmon, mackerel, and sardines was always on board. Fresh meat and poultry were usually optional, unless available along the way, but fresh ocean fish was preferred.

"Dense, chewy whole grain breads were carried, plus a special flour mix of whole wheat, buckwheat, and oats for making pancakes."

"Hey man," barks Theodore, "how about those pork sausages we would kill (a pig) for?"

"Aye, Theodore, you've revealed my sins of omission!" replies the man, "I admit that I love breakfast flapjacks and sausages. But these sausages are without nitrites or preservatives, and each cooked portion is less than three ounces. Besides, I frequently purchase ground lean pork and mix it with fresh sage and other herbs, and a small amount of salt.

"Our powerhouse breakfasts depended on pancakes more than sausages. The batter lends itself to a thousand variations in the interest of good nutrition and digestion. The basic batter consists of 2 cups of mixed grains flour, 1 large egg, 0.5 teaspoon of baking soda, 3 tablespoons olive oil, 0.5 cup milk powder, ad lib water with vigorous stirring for desired consistency and then add 0.25 cup cider vinegar (reacts with baking soda to produce carbon dioxide for leavening). From this point on, you are on your own. You can add chopped dates, raisins, fresh berries, grated pears, apples - everything works!

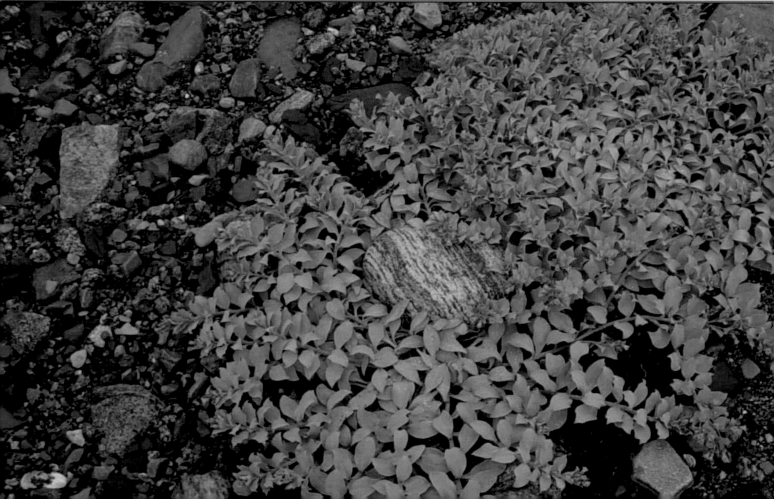

"Lest you consider this a Spartan diet, we carried an ample supply of raw nuts, dried fruits, fruit juices, but no sodas -- I could go on and on. Snacking was not allowed to be excessive, or to replace regular meals," the man insists, "and we carried and drank lots of potable water, but couldn't keep Theodore from lapping puddles and streams.

"Perhaps he sought those cedar-water flavors to make up for the lack of condiments in our diet. Years ago, travelers in Labrador commented on the absence of spices, other than pepper, in the average diet", recalls the man. "People in harsh environments have big appetites for basic foods and no perceived need for flavor enhancement. At least some of the demand for spices and artificial flavors can be attributed to overstuffed bodies and jaded appetites.

"A healthy appetite brings sharp awareness of the flavor and aroma of each cooking ingredient, so Theodore and I learned to depend mostly on pepper, with an occasional boost from a single spice mixture (Mrs. Dash Salt-free Seasoning Blend).

"Regularity was an essential part of our regimen," says the man, "meals were kept on schedule, three times a day, starting with breakfast at daybreak and a long walk. Even while traveling long distances, there was adequate allowance for rest stops, meals, and exercise. An early breakfast provides a long day to meet every requirement, and the summertime far north contributed many additional daylight hours."

"Fair warning!" barks Theodore, "your gentle readers are about to boil over. Ominous muttering in the ranks, talk of a deep fat fryer rebellion."

"Never thought I'd have to tell mid-lifers how to cook, but the deep fat fryer and barbeque are so deeply entrenched everywhere. Many Oriental people place heavy reliance on rice cookers. Basic models are convenient and inexpensive, and can be used to cook wheat kernels and other whole grains, as well as brown rice. Attractive meals can be produced by adding chopped up vegetables, seafood, or meats as the grains are being cooked in water, or the cooked rice or other grains can be covered with a delicious stir-fry.

"Leftover cooked rice or grains can be mixed into the pancake batter, for breakfast, or used to thicken and add substance to soups."

"GRUEL!" whines Theodore, "I ain't no orphan who's expected to live on porridge. Sounds like 'gruel-i-ty' to animals."

"Thanks, Theodore, you've said the magic word - *porridge*," replies the man, "the grains cooked in water or broths are completely versatile and at least can be used as nourishing thickeners to replace the empty calorie starches and gums that are frequently used. Moreover, a porridge can appear on the table as chili, gumbo, seafood chowder, beef stew. Yesterday, Theodore, we shared an oyster stew, thickened with oatmeal! Need I say more?

"The wok is also an ingenious cooking utensil, shaped for efficient heat transfer, but it is frequently allowed to overheat and damage fats before the other ingredients are added," says the man. "My variation, in starting a stir-fry, is to cut up and combine onions, mushrooms, ginger, garlic, strips of meat, with a small amount of olive oil.

"I place the mixture in the wok and apply medium heat while stirring constantly. At the first sign of scorching I add soy sauce and a tablespoon of water. Evaporation of this added water and the water content of the vegetables limits the temperature and protects the oil."

"Old man speaks with forked tongue," barks Theodore, "I saw him grease that big, high-sided fry pan, and no water in sight."

"Oh for the good old days, when dogs didn't yap," sighs the man, "yes, I apply gentle heat to that flat-bottomed, non-stick skillet and grease it by quickly sliding a stick of butter over its surface. The amount of butter used is minimal, and it seems safe and suited for this purpose. Then I pour pancake batter on this surface heated sufficiently to allow browning. In much the same way, boiled then sliced potatoes can be lightly pan-fried and allowed to form thin crusts.

"I'm glad you mentioned this high-sided fry pan, Theodore," the man continues, "note that it has a tight-fitting lid. An infinite variety of complete meals can be prepared in this utensil, starting with about one-half inch of water to produce steam. Meats, poultry, or fish can be kept off the bottom with a perforated metal plate, and a variety of fresh vegetables can fill up much of the remaining space. Usually, such meals can simmer for an hour and be ready to eat.

"Many of these food combinations, especially when chicken joints are used, produce wonderful broths. These should be refrigerated, the fats skimmed off, and the underlying liquid saved to flavor other dishes, including soups.

"I could go on and on, but you, my gentle readers, have many more years to develop your own cooking protocols than I have. However, I must again remind you not to overlook the SEEDS.

"Take your time about shopping for a mill to grind brown rice, chick peas, buckwheat, dried green beans, millet, mung beans, oats, pinto beans, rye, soybeans, and wheat, since this suitable equipment is expensive. Meanwhile, buy the prepared flours from reliable suppliers and get in the habit of using them. But keep in mind that stored flours rapidly lose important nutritional values, so sooner or later, you will want to get all the benefits the seeds have to offer.

"I am the proud owner of a grain mill," boosts the man, "and have made tasty, compact loaves of bread with my bread-making machine. But to be honest, I prefer the simplicity and flexibility of pancakes. A large batch can be used each morning for a whole week, with different fruits, berries and nuts, added daily for variety.

"Healthful additions to breads and pancakes can be just a few tablespoons of freshly ground seeds of almonds, flax, sunflower, or walnuts, all of which contain valuable oils. A small high-speed blade coffee grinder will deal with these fatty seeds, and are not expensive to buy if you do not have one."

The man apologetically addresses his audience, "Sorry, mates, I must now stop this cooking lesson and depend on you to expand upon it to satisfy your own needs. I've frequently observed in supermarkets how spoiled and child-like people act when they seriously debate what they want for dinner. To embark on a long-range longevity plan, plainly and simply, you'll have to mature and make adult decisions concerning longevity food selections. You have lots of time to rearrange priorities, but Father Time is keeping tabs.

"If you approach these concepts slowly and responsibly, I can assure you that your newly acquired preferences will provide as much eating pleasure as before. Because, as the lady said when she kissed the cow, 'It's simply a matter of taste.'"

INTEGRATION

The sacredness of private integrity.
—Ralph Waldo Emerson

"For now, we must turn our backs on the reassuring clatter of pots and pans, and discuss more devastating hazards than eating damaging foods," says the man.

"'Devastating' sounds scary," snivels Theodore, "what can be worse than eating yourself to death?"

"Far worse, Theodore, because the damage is spiritual instead of corporeal. It involves the act of conferring *invisibility* upon a large segment of the population. *'Ageism'* is a communicable, <u>mindset disease</u> that is endemic in our world, and keeps much of the older population separate from everyday society.

"I seriously doubt that our leaders, our courts, and our electorate have ever taken the time to examine and fully comprehend the meaning of *'Integration'* and the citizen's rights that it implies. *Integration is the making up or composition of a whole, by adding together, or combining, the separate parts.*

"*Integration* – when illuminated by such words as affiliation, amalgamation, assimilation, combination, consolidation, desegregation, oneness and wholeness - indicates agreement, if not awareness, that the ultimate goal of human civilization is *oneness and wholeness* with each other, and with Mother Earth.

"These meaningful words cascade and swirl through my head," says the man. "As a certified chow hound, such words as 'oneness' and 'wholeness' make me think of *food*. We are what we eat, and Mother Earth feeds us, so there's logic in encouraging the growing and marketing of organic foods.

"Organic foods are not only an added safeguard to our health, but provide us with an opportunity to support the whole concept of sustainable farming, home industries, and elimination of chemicals from our food supply. Is organic farming economically feasible? In the long run will it be economically feasible to forget our *oneness* with Mother Earth and let her be destroyed?

"While traveling in Alberta, I met a professor who teaches economics at a well-known university. Without malice aforethought, I commented, 'Oh! You teach that *evil science!*'

"I expressed my concern that uncontrolled expansion of human activities are devastating the planet, while governments, prodded by lobbyists and the tacit approval of economists, aim for continued increases in Gross National Product, as the desired, ultimate goal of our civilization.

"If the <u>bottom line</u> continues to be our primary driving force, then don't expect this hard-edged, selfish system of governance to have the slightest regard for old people who are confined to their own lonely worlds and kept separated from this swinging, upward-moving, pretending-to-be-integrated society.

"I resent those occasions when, after what appeared to be pleasant socializing with middle-aged people, they have suddenly suggested that I team up with a parent who is unhappy and bored," says the man. "I've heard that insult directed at a child who tries to hang out with adults and is told to 'play with someone your own age'.

"When this occurs, I long to tell them how hard it is to remain visible in this uncaring world, to avoid exactly what their parent is experiencing as an outcast from normal, everyday life.

"In my travels I've met hundreds of older people who share my feelings. They avoid segregation by mingling with the transient population. Somehow people around a campfire are much more friendly and tolerant.

"Sorry, me Hearties, no quick fix, but forewarned is forearmed," says the man, "but there's strength in numbers if you have the will to exert your influence, to insist on your right to remain integrated in society -- twenty, thirty, even forty years from now. Until then, integration will remain an unrealized dream, until some drastic awareness of priorities produces a government that can provide equal treatment for each and every citizen, and the survival of all."

SOCIALIZATION

Socialization - A continuous process whereby an individual acquires a personal identity and learns the norms, values, behavior and social skills appropriate to his or her social position -Webster's Encyclopedic Unabridged Dictionary of the English Language (1996), Random House, New York City

"Appropriate to <u>your</u> social position?" fang-grins Theodore. "Don't go hoity-toity on me, old man. Been a long time since I've seen you live in anything but that barn on EarthWise Farm, this Newfoundland cabin, and our GMC Van en route to elsewhere."

"That's the point, dummy dawg," replies the man, "this extra lease on life from age seventy-six to eighty-nine - a gift of fate, genetics, or pure piss and vinegar-has tightened my perceptions and loosened my reactions. Yea man, Theodore, I'm increasingly intolerant of pomp, circumstance, and stupidity, especially when I see resource-wasting overblown housing springing up everywhere except on Newfoundland's Northern Peninsula, where the homes are usually functional and unpretentious."

"How about that yukky-tasting necktie, I chewed up several years ago? Can't you tie on a better taste than that?" asks Theodore.

"Chokers are just another encumbrance I choose to ignore, brother Theo. Them city dudes need 'em to restrict the flow of polluted air.

"What do they know about Shallow Bay Beach with its daybreak sunrises, cloud displays, color changes, and double rainbows? My throat must be free to gasp wonder at the unique privilege of being there. Man and dog alone walk this three-mile half-circle beach staring into the very heart of the weather map, its stratospheric isobars marked by colors gaudily splashed over three hundred and sixty degrees of magnificent sky.

"*Simone de Beauvoir's book, The Coming of Age,* was mentioned in the preface as relevant to the situations elderly persons still encounter, a third of a century after her book was written. She described how a number of famous people dealt with old age, many of whom were unable to consider it any better than an incurable fatal disease. In spite of such depressing reactions, most of them valued each remaining day on earth.

"This dismal outlook need not apply to *your* generation of middle-aged persons, dear reader, but you are indeed the next victims of *ageism* if you refuse to demand your citizen rights tooth and nail."

"Oh my," grins Theodore, as the man gingerly climbs on the cabin table, "you poor more-or-less-fifty-year-oldsters are in for another harangue, this time the old skipper thinks he's Admiral Farragut!"

"Bo's'n," the man shouts at Theodore, "damn the Torpedoes! Assemble crew with life jackets on poop deck, Go! Go!

"Be not afraid, me Hearties," soothes the man, *"ageism* won't drown you if you are man or woman enough to face it head-on. But if you are too chicken-livered to run the course, now is the time to join that deep fat fryer – OVERBOARD!

"Now my brave mates, hear me out," continues the man, "as I watch the passage of waves, I see them as one human generation after another, driven like sheep by forces they cannot control, until they crash and disappear. But I have seen run-outs along the deep water beaches of the Atlantic, where waves refuse loss of identify and form a powerful outward bound current with a life of its own.

"Equally powerful forces in society can determine our fates, but keep in mind that your generation will control a numerically strong segment of the votes, and can remain an active, aggressive part of society if you are physically and mentally up to it.

"As I see it, Mates, an average person in this society has the potential to mature for a whole lifetime, but all too often the process is delayed and overburdened by family care, the pressures of ambition, and making a living. "So many mid-lifers then want to rest on their laurels, indulge in fun and games, and forget that the most interesting, character-determining years may still lie ahead. A time to mature, if mental and physical capabilities remain active."

Human brains and bowels are involuntary tissues that cannot abide laziness and neglect. To stay clear of the bone yard, keep 'em active!

VISIBILITY

"ONLY IN NEWFOUNDLAND . . . would I have accepted Hank as my guide, when I met him, on this lonely road!" says the man. "He offered to lead me to the John Farwell farm. Suddenly, Theodore was nowhere to be found, then appeared out of thick brush with a moose leg (left by hunters) in his mouth.

"Hank obligingly separated moose leg from dog, then led us down a wet, stony roadway, bounded by dense forest, to John Farwell's farm."

John Farwell, born in Port au Choix eighty-two years ago, has been married to Rita for over fifty years. He developed and actively operates this two-hectare (about 5 acres) farm, fenced to keep out marauding animals from the surrounding forest.

His wonderful, organically raised vegetables are readily sold by the Farwell store and other food outlets.

The remarkable fertility of this farm can be attributed to John's use of locally available organic matter, which he estimates has included 400 tons of kelp, 25 tons of shrimp waste and 25 tons of chicken manure mixed with sawdust.

Rita Farwell, born in Port au Choix eighty-three years ago, each day attends church where she serves as a Eucharist Minister, and performs other duties as well. She manages the Farwell Store and keeps its shelves stocked with interesting craftworks, delicious preserves, John's prime-fresh vegetables and other staples.

The above pictures show the inside and outside of the Farwell Store. In her wonderfully functional kitchen, where the author was royally treated and permitted to sample her cakes, pie, preserves and a chutney which used rhubarb as its basic ingredient.

Sunsets can be every bit as Perfect as Sunrises

The Newfoundland-Ontario-North Carolina Connection

The text and photography in this book are the result of a cooperative effort that took place two thousand miles from the author's home in Ocean, North Carolina, where he was director of Marine Chemurgics, a research laboratory devoted to complete utilization of fish and shellfish.

Editor Gerry Lavery, from Simcoe, Ontario, admits her age makes her eligible for the lifestyle the book recommends. She is a promising candidate because she is adventurous, (a retired sky-diver), and up to her keister in university courses as well as a dedicated traveler.

Technical Consultant Lorne Warren of Parson's Pond, Newfoundland, has managed the *wildegeest.com* and *bestfrienddog.com* web domains for several years, has recently recorded the entire WILDEGEEST! book on CD, and prepared the text and images in this Sequel to meet the digital printing requirements of the publisher. He has been a teacher since 1976. His duties have now been expanded to include distance education. He also operates a company called Netcreations, Inc.

৵৶৵৶৵৶৵৶৵৶৵৶৵৶৵৶৵৶৵৶৵৶৵৶

Live Seed Diet Program

Something old and something new, a combination of the tried and true, and a fresh outlook on basic foods and gentler food preparation methods that may lengthen your life.

Seed Money - The author's proceeds from this book will help operate EarthWise Farm

Management Committee -Gerry Lavery, Lorne Warren, and Todd Hiscock (Cow Head, Nfld.)

This demonstration of a sustainable farming operation begins its third year with plans to expand acreage and use of cover crops, chickens in moveable enclosures (chicken tractors) and other measures for soil improvement; to prove the feasibility of producing pesticide-free fruits, vegetables and grains; to demonstrate kitchen equipment for grinding whole grains and the direct use of the fresh flours in tasty recipes, and how to cook and derive full benefits from whole grains, without grinding.

The two World Wide Web domains, www.wildegeest.com and www.bestfrienddog.com will issue frequent reports concerning these activities with emphasis on findings which may be relevant to the promising organic farming potential of Newfoundland.

KEEP IN TOUCH!

Printed in the United States
by Baker & Taylor Publisher Services